ENDLESS
RUNNING GAMES

BY
GARETH DURASOW

Published by
Dog Horn Publishing
45 Monk Ings, Birstall, Batley WF17 9HU
United Kingdom
doghornpublishing.com

ISBN 978-1-907133-90-9
Cover artwork by
Mike Barrett

Typesetting by
Adam Lowe

UK Distribution: Central Books
99 Wallis Road, London, E9 5LN, United Kingdom
orders@centralbooks.com
Phone:+44 (0) 845 458 9911
Fax: +44 (0) 845 458 9912

Overseas Distribution: Printondemand-worldwide.com
9 Culley Court
Orton Southgate
Peterborough
PE2 6XD
Telephone: 01733 237867
Facsimile: 01733 234309
Email: info@printondemand-worldwide.com

First Edition published by Dog Horn Publishing, 2015

ENDLESS RUNNING GAMES

Acknowledgements

The author would like to thank Adam Strickson for his help with editing this collection.

Acknowledgements are due to the editors of the following publications:

Angel Exhaust, Anything Anymore Anywhere, Cadaverine, Eunoia Review, The French Literary Review, The Grist Anthology of New Writing (Grist Books), *Leeds Debacle, LS13* (Dead Ink), *The New Victoria/Odeon Anthology* (The New Fire Tree Press), *Openned, PANK, Polluto, The Red Ceilings, The Rialto, Shearsman, The State of the Arts, Sunfish.*

Thanks also to Matthew Hedley Stoppard and Richard Smyth for their feedback, Vitalija Lukoseviciene for her collaboration on 'Poetui', and David Devanny for typesetting 'Love Poem from Garry Kasparov'.

for Alex Durasow
—both of them

CONTENTS

A NOTE ON MY SOURCES:

A. Alvarez (*Beckett*). Capcom (*Super Street Fighter IV*). Jimi Hendrix ('Voodoo Chile'). Ludmila I. (a prospective Russian bride). Kazuo Koike (*Lone Wolf and Cub*). Jacques Rivière (correspondence between Artaud and Rivière). Dylan Thomas (*Under Milk Wood*). Treyarch (*Call of Duty Black Ops 2*). Yamamoto Tsunetomo (*Hagakure*).

'I don't know one damned butterfly from another
my ignorance of the stars is formidable'
—John Berryman, *Dream Song 265*

'I'm afraid to eat sandwiches I've made myself because they always have
blood in them.'
—Jeremy Clarkson, *Top Gear*

1. Games with the Dead

THE AUBREY BEARDSLEY COLOURING BOOK

—no end to the chapter of blood

1

It is not for the dog-walker alone to stumbleupon murder
nor a blood-spatter analyst to scrutinise the platter

to determine the point at which hair stops running
an artery drops the baton

all bodies of water are a kind of tombola
just put in your hand (or paw)

and with green sleeves
perhaps you'll unsheathe Excalibur

from the algal bloom,
perhaps a head if you're bobbing for apples.

2

Enter Lavinia. She knows why boys make the best machine gun noises.
Blow in their faces, bang them together

but persevere, their eyes will open and fix on you
that's the moment to plant the kiss,

not the lips, God forbid
some will spit a gift horse in the mouth

and you don't want blood on your pearly whites
but most are thrilled, the look in their eyes

before they close or fall to the floor
and this is how we roll,

not braying nails into coffin lids
but pilot hole, clearance hole, countersink.

3

Isolde loves him not without the drink
the wounds that make an al fresco croak of him

Tristan loves her slim so he can imprison her wrists
in manacles of little finger and thumb

What will be found in the den of her tresses,
of she who doesn't bother keeping up with her roots

Under the carnations, ladybirds rove
a spattering of colour that just had to be red.

4

Compelled to kick the objects washed up on the beach
wheel trims, human feet

the kind of rose for which you barter
and the head falls off at the very first sniff

you have to throw in your mobile phone
engagement ring

if you want to win more than just a handful of silt
to shunt a shipwreck from the front of the shelf

to win back your runaway (or one just like them)
from the teddy bear pedlars, their underhand arithmetic.

PRAYER FOR EDWARD KENWAY

Across your outfit
a seminar in butchery,
the manpower required
to fillet Leviathan.
How many carcasses
weighted on all sides
itch to fly,
to preserve their bones
and maternal instinct.
It's in their code to be game,
an earthquake padlocked
onto my heart
when a live one breaches,
its aftershock
beneath the city of my scalp
and the seabed
reassembled by crustaceans,
clawed things
the names of which
I cannot tell you,
a flash mob of detritivores
making good use of
a man-o-war's hand-me-downs.
Earth will eat them raw;
sludge recalling Neptune's acres,
a worthier life to be had ashore
where sirens are a novelty.
Take as long as you like at your bookcase,
take an Odyssey.

Edward James Kenway (1693—1735) is the protagonist of Assassin's
Creed IV: Black Flag, *a historical action-adventure video game.*

Prayers for Captain Ahab

'...to the last I grapple with thee; from hell's heart I stab at thee;
for hate's sake I spit my last breath at thee.'

'I don't care who you are,
here's to your dream.'
—Surfer, Guinness advert, 1999

1

Here's to you, Ahab,
all hands clenched beneath the lengthening night
quagmired in wedlock
with the dearth of wives to be trawled from the seabed,
sown under your fingernails
the dry death privilege of select few lice,
white your knuckles atop the wheel
till something's got to break.
On thy lips, what name quivers?
What regret the relentless bite?
There is no quarry to be wagered on here
save the horses that outride us and the skeletons beneath.
Anemones play a slow kind of kiss-catch
in the skull's brain cavity.
What will you do when the dead have clogged the sea?
When they have clogged the sea,
I will toast to their freedom
with bacchanalian hiccups
but responsibly, with a candle for the *Baywatch* babes,
its eyelashes aflutter, its whale fat tongue
crackling beneath the indolence of the stars,
the comets you pick, lick, roll n' flick
as Hale-Bopp comes to try her luck again.
Ever seen those brine-beaked corbies unzip a fish's gizzard?
Such panache. Gelatine of eyeball clogging their craws.
That feeling of encore
when a Cherokee slazengers your face
with a tomahawk.

2

"There she blows!" will light a fire under their arses,
thy weather-stripping howl in the grand ballroom of skellywags
and now we are caught in the midst of their danse macabre
swept up by their momentum as the horse sea balks,

the vessel roars like an accordion of tar
the bluishturfgoneblack
now the moon has had a stroke
the crew in frenzy and pissed as stoats.

You have to put your eyeballs on sale,
your limbs, your vestiges of sense
as Belzebuth gears up his rollicking shanty,
seesaws in the ballroom to the mad mad capering of surfers' bones.

3

You lifted your head
the sea rushed to occupy the hell of your mouth
more salty more disgusting than a ladle of sperm
and I heard you cry out upon the Earth—

Something grapple
Something stab
Something breath.

REGINA LISSO

Regina, you've such Fabergé teeth,
the very pietà the Third Reich deserves
coiffure disheveled by furtive caresses
gaunt young men compelled to touch.

Permission to sit with her awhile
to defibrillate her with my eyes
a kiss so voltaic
her needlepoint hands unfurl and

Vogue
all over my roughshod face,
nurse's fingers gone to waste,
their vestiges of dexterity

unpick a button from the upholstery
like a girl chastised in the fairy wing repair shop
plucks out an offensive eye
to sleep more soundly in the sun's black spot.

*Regina Lisso was a member of the German Red Cross. She committed
suicide to avoid capture by US troops. Her body was photographed by the
American photographer Lee Miller.*

Prayers for Inglarious Bostards

1

Rosie the Riveter,
Cleopatra for the machine age,
the Gaga of war bonds, in at number one
with the kind of song that arrives unbidden
while you're bleeding out, taking potshots at a Tiger tank.
Gentlemen, I bring you the honey to envisage
if you get shit-scared in the bottleneck to Normandy,
in battleship emulsion frolicking like a harlot
a chorus of go-go munitionettes in back,
the leopard-skin corps, they reek of TNT
smokin' hot shellshock canary grrls next door
breaking out their hairnets and peekaboo basques
to keep your eyes front and your cock in your hands,
a kiss more sticky than a zeppelin of blood
to bless the trajectory of every round they touch.

2

On his back with the gullet of Troy in his teeth
Hectares of resistance and Hector to his name
Now is not the time for an origami Hurricane
Get him to the chopper!
Over the page could be a picture trap,
a mugshot of Jaws
or a boy with a cleft palate,
the shock of the overleaf
processed in the time a dartboard's wounds take to close,
that's what young readers of Warlord missed out on.
Get this man a medevac
Say it's just a flesh wound, say 'tis but a scratch,
that they couldn't hit a priest on a mountain of sugar.
Army ants have the mandibles we need
Tear it off at the thorax
Hey presto, you've fashioned yourself a nifty suture.

3

In back of the Crimea the last scrum of dysentery has been kicked into
                        touch
but the cutting edge tactics are a throwback to the Somme
Lay down your corpses to be your walls
Lay down your corpses to bridge the moat
Attack your enemies on the bodies of comrades
and victory will be yours;
tin pot hats, lucky hipflasks
filched from the bog and the pockets therein.
Time gentlemen please
time yon pillocks went face-planting homewards
crabways alone
a-rorping a ribaldrous love song.

POEM TOWARDS 7 MILLION HITS

after Nokia N96

To play ping-pong with Bruce Lee
That is a very good way to lose your teeth.
If Bruce Lee asks whether he would hesitate
To gouge out your eyes—the man who gave you a hiding last night
If you are partially sighted, sparring to a soundtrack of cheesy jazz
Your feeble roundhouse and clumsy side kick
If Bruce Lee instructs you to relate to him
Don't move just for the sake of moving
Try to feel the wind blowing
Can you hear the birdsong? the dog's bark in the distance?
Could it be that your boss's lip just burst
That their neck gave way to a swift application of superhuman torque
The expression on Bruce Lee's face one to practise while slaughtering chickens
Unless you like your patio furniture better with yourself among it
I suggest you do as he says and empty your cup
But don't hold a kick pad up to Bruce Lee
If someone with a moustache is standing behind you
And if you're the one with the moustache, invited by Bruce Lee
                    to touch Bruce Lee
It's going to end badly for one of your kneecaps
If you go outside to find Bruce Lee waiting in your garden
If he has assumed a casual stance by the water feature
If he is eating a packet of crisps, jacket slung over his shoulder
And you hold aloft a pair of green parakeets in a Chinese bird cage
Just don't, not even with knives—and certainly not one at a time
Maybe if you narrow your eyes and your feet take the time
                    to find their place in the grass
Maybe then you'll be able to touch Bruce Lee
But if you do manage a touch, make it a touch that doesn't
                    rip his clothes, a touch that doesn't make him bleed.

PRAYERS FOR ANAKIN SKYWALKER

1

Every dandelion knew him, knew to be braced for its brains blown out.
The woods he used to roam resorted to scorched earth tactics
burning its mattresses, cushions and pushchairs
to stop thinking of him, the way that he was
a little boy, dog-happy in the loaf-thick snow
mistaking sandbags for piglets asleep at the roadside
carrying a baguette like a pole-arm all the way home
Just the height to be clotheslined by your wing mirror
How he clambered staircases of waterfowl in flight,
trapezed the vapours of Red Arrows out to pasture
besmirching the name of any cloud he liked,
painting the shells of local snails
to know them on return, to know which were loyal to him,
never seeing his hands when he dreamt.

2

Night rain,
a sky tearing arrows out of itself,
the stratosphere veneered with a zinc complexion.
Flashes of flak,
your popcorn at critical.
Starships failing at obtuse angles.
THX has a field day—
orchestral manoeuvers,
turbolaser pwnage.
The force of greater numbers and budget
g-hardened,
eating Gs like Jesus is their copilot,
gunned for by the beaks of lens and boom mic
or firing from the hip
with murder in his eyes.
If you peer into the visor there's a Māori inside,
stubble set to heavy,
teeth to coup de grâce,
life lines identical from palm to palm,
the famous pride of the mechanised Republic,
the military brightness of bugle and drum.

3

The Force that formerly you held in bridle
now a bounding, ferocious beast
crazy and ready to slaughter, to devastate
to engorge between toilet breaks,
Stumbras the hammer, pillow the anvil
for the nailing of horseshoes onto your skull,
an era in boiling, the Force of the present
anger to something, hate to whatever.
The Force, it is a hurricane
it sluices your blood through the wildest boar,
cuts and shuts the heart of a wrestler
to the chassis of a beetle.
Looking over your son's shoulder
how would you like to hear him say
it's you he's busy drawing;
a stickman in black
and vigorous crayon.

TELEGRAM FROM TRALFAMADORE

That theirs was the conscience round
one could ascertain from the kickback

but the burning man is not a samizdat
the hanging man no pear.

Better a bullet breach the cardiac
muscle through a hipflask,

property of Private Eddie Slovik
back against the wall

condemned for the brass he stole
when he was just a kid.

Tralfamadore is the fictional planet from the novel Slaughterhouse-Five *by Kurt Vonnegut.*

LOVE POEM FOR ELLEN RIPLEY

Old girl, I am made of Rolls-Royce and snake bones.
I scream in the key of flank-gorged spears,
of a steam train's brakes as it hits you in the chest
with force enough to fire your blood
onto the shower screen, were it not for the critter
for which your lungs make good birthday cake.
From some kind of crawl-space
I want you between my innermost lips
to lift you by the lapels irrevocably into a vent shaft
where a cameraman lies on his belly, dying to see
what an intermittent blip looks like in the flesh.

LOVE POEM FROM GARRY KASPAROV

```
#include <stdio.h>
#include <math.h>
int love()
{

printf(
        "To sit down with you
        shake hands without proxy/n");
gets(you);

printf(
        "and take you apart, before the clock strikes twelve
        and you're an abacus in the dark/n");
gets (dark);
strcat(you,dark);

        I(in turn){ being human =
        "ascribing glitches to higher intelligence" +
        "oblivious to what makes you tick"
         (at_tangents) { at times to my detriment++ }
        };

if(lights_on>lights_off)
{printf(

        "so few of us with the lights on
        many of those with nobody home/n");
gets(nobody);
}
while(lights_on>lights_off)
{printf(

        'so few of us in the know
        about what thought did exactly./n');

};
return 0;
}
```

Bin Bagged

—*The Sun, 3rd May 2011*

This one's for Hoppo, gone too soon
with the name of the boy who put soap in our fishpond.

He's out of the game, mate
skull a bit breezier, voice of a seashell

an ace in a deck of most wanted crazies
who cannot imagine an indoor ski slope

who believe in a mouse that leaves a coin under their pillow
for every round they fire at the sky.

There's always summat.
Ten across, vengeful justice (2,3,3,2,3).

Confederate troops arrayed in ranks of moderate rock
build a McDonald's from the blood clot up.

FOR THE LAST FLAT CAPPER

The last flat cap, worn unto death by Castleford's pantheon
faces black as the seams they dreamt of
relentless beside their wives
slate grey from lives spent stoking

men in repose behind bastion walls
made of pint pot embossed with their names
and ceramic ashtrays now for shelling nuts.
A grown man cried when sent to smoke in the open air

deceased in all but his John Smith's arm mechanism
his winding wheel of reminiscence.
I'll remember him after the rings have been unscrewed from his knuckles,
the roll-up filched from behind his ear, the gold tooth levered from his rictus.

2. Notes for Future Sonnets

—FROM A LINE
BY H P LOVECRAFT

April brought a kind of madness to the country folk
thawing inside their marital cauls
dust mites fossilised in the sinus coral
eyes open like jpegs
the moment a bee slits its saccharine belly.
'Gotta go nan, am totally pissed,'
said the girl on the train from several seats behind,
so petite she could of died
had that empty can of Rubicon
come rolling by again.
To let her hold my hand
meant gambling her fingers.
I wonder if she made it all the way to Rochdale,
I wonder if she made it all the way to Christmas.

When you grow up, will you conduct a symphony or steam trains
or descend like a disco ball underneath the anvil with the hammerheads
Will you plant the kiss of life upon a grandmother clock
rescued from a skip, stuck mid-slap across the chops
to the numeral next in line to wash its hands of us,
to chop it down with the edge of its hand
the mountain you make out of a milk tooth.
Cloned from the muck on your dad's guitar strings,
are you preordained to audit the stuff soaking up the pavement;
a glove, a glove, a leaf, a glove,
to pull your weight like the tank engine you loved
with his moon face and capacity to sneeze,
so if ever you lose an arm, no-one pities the ease
with which it's picked up off the floor and carried to triage.

We affront our dads and their razor of choice. Pastors of the foam
                    and most deliberate genuflection
How they regard us, their looks askance in misted mirrors
Our nails too precious, cuticles too soft to see Subbuteo through
                    to injury time
Our schooling and temperament detrimental to one's ability to work
                    like a man
Our every muse a spanner in his ball sack.
Was ever he aroused by the blurb on a Rimbaud Collected
('…his stormy affair…', '…nomadic adventures…'
how what starts with a barber ends up in the heliotropes)
or compelled to write on the woodchip intended to muffle
the clangers we drop in our washing up bowls.
Do they think to appropriate wooden dowels from the workplace
for the purpose of knocking them into our ear 'oles
driving home the sense to keep our most lucrative fingers
far from the teeth of his circular saw.

When I woke up with the gas and air bends and a bowl for my blood
the dentist asked, 'Would you like to take your teeth home?'
then after a fortnight when I opened that vial
I knew what He-Man smelt whenever Skeletor cackled or screamed in his face
Just a few keepsakes that went out with the ark
A pink drumming bunny when you have a surname like mine
Does every kid in school get a little red book
or New Testament and Psalms
Weather permitting
A full power station view
Ferrybridge, Eggborough, Drax—you choose
Tomorrow another day, with a full contingent of charge
Breakfast on the move, swallow it bodily, bun the lot
and walk towards whatever dandelion seeds could be so afraid of.

O sweet entrant from country with
higher incidence of tuberculosis,
your daily routine; adhering stickers to cardboard sleeves,
to slice liver and put plastic to the torch
My queen of the slatwall bend,
the extent of your malice a curse along the lines
I hope your rabbit dies and you can't sell the hutch
My sleeping file-sharer,
how ruthless you are at freeing up disk space
How you drag and drop A Beautiful Mind into the recycle bin
straight at the credits
and by committing this to paper
I betray you
to the Federation Against Copyright Theft.

—FOR 'THE NORTON ANTHOLOGY OF POEMS ABOUT LOVERS WHO TURN OUT TO BE CATS (OR CATS WHO TURN OUT TO BE LOVERS)'

He batters the kill, unravels its best laid plans of intestinal tract
like a skein of wool across the grass, makes off with the rest
bibbed with blood up brickwork so sheer
that Sisyphus, this close to throwing in the towel
regards his albatross a stone's throw from a lark
and Jacob Marley perseveres inside a locksmith's wet dream
grateful that at least his burden doesn't bleed.
No belfry rings for the kill, just the bell around his throat
when he explodes in a fission of maths,
fathoming the vertices between here and home.
He shuns the limelight indulging the strays
applauded by the doors of bleak estates
and returns to a yard anointed with piss
where koi carps' heckles go unheard.

Back when I lived I lived off the platinum hairs unearthed in my mouth
the ones that fell from the pin-up girl above my bed
Blu-Tack crucifiction fit for the nose on a flying fortress
strafed across the midriff
by the brains of Willy Messerschmitt.
I chased double-yellow lines down the drain
after butterfingered coppers
invested in teapigs
at the café where Dogsbody drummed on the counter
expecting the cutlery to show she's the fairest,
while a gnat alighted, primed to complete
the rose behind her ear
then drunk on ink by the tenth of a teaspoon
tucked itself into the rapid zap.

The night we wore our 3D glasses home
with a taxi for a monoplex,
electrons with legs
impacted on the screen
every car a seashell in confession
ambulances lost us the way balloons lose their children,
your smile like Batgirl's
should ever she smile or hiccup
when out on a caper,
tab-ends left to the slipstream
dreamt of metamorphosing into Penny Blacks,
last known whereabouts; under a pylon's heel
Too many suspects arrayed in the night
like Vitruvian hulks.

Back when I lived, it seems like yesterday
I opened my dictionary on Diagram/Diamondback moth
and dry pressed rose petals fell out onto the floor.
One can never look too surprised,
sanding eyebrows to sawdust and starting from scratch,
drawing them a little higher than the last.
In the bath, shaving her legs, a minor nick,
blood unravelled like your favourite cassette
and she, A positive, couldn't care less
because as we all know, A blood types shouldn't eat meat.
This and other factoids one overhears on the lash.
Did you know eighty percent of men cry in their cars?
O little X-File, who lovingly pushed my cuticles back into place,
the coroner's verdict on this procedure: Mickey Mouse.

Lying in the grass, resting my head on *The Elek Book of Oriental Verse,*
we do the voices of Ernie and Bert
saying hey to the clouds,
hey to the trees
the remains of an insect smeared overleaf
eating from the o in pension as the pages closed in
uninvited into a narrow escape,
we laugh at the names our respective countries
have given to the noises that animals make.
My kingdom for a net for the catching of kigo words,
the sound of a buttercup under my chin
a football so trusting it eats from her hand
as we watch the dogfight of butterflies
rooting for the red one.

3. Games with the Living

POEM FOR TESTING YOUR VISION

Now we have reached the trees—the beautiful trees!
their roots in someone's casket
contracting from the soil a human wilt,
bark aspiring to marble,
trunk to Venus de Milo
and to that end wishes lightning to strike twice
to drape their arms across car windscreens
the tiara they proffer no tiara at all
but the jaw they grew up with,
the memory of birdsong as it sounded before
laughter and smoke alarms,
rifle report
of a child advancing
plastic battalions
blasting snails into rubble and slag
happy as Ginsberg in Bunting's lap
we'll be together at the end of the Stelliferous Age
building a sandbank with our pension of skin,
gifted to the Westerlies, encrusting guitar strings.

GUN SONG

Dad says they'll sew p'tatas in my ear 'oles,
grownups in a tree house. Guess Who faces.

Elitism of clay shoots. Erections in the cordite
chamber. Recalibrate the trap pull crack

Kickback knackers his shoulder for life
so every clay pigeon has a fighting chance

Break the action, a bare fist tracheotomy
The empties make good finger mice

But as for pen lids and Lego bricks
nothing's going near my mouth again

till Amy, backlit on a bear rug in front of the telly
takes off her bra in the hiddenness of sound.

HORATIO IN MY POCKET

after Hamletmachine

—NO PART FOR YOU IN THIS MY TRAGEDY

I am Horatio,
the one denied a mortal swig
who envenomed steel never took.
Back when you lived I killed a snapdragon thus;
pinched its throat between thumb and forefinger
to play the ventriloquist next to your ear—
handsome devil, may I tear off some bread
and scatter it among thy quarrel of ducks?
Ignore uncle knobhead on matters such as the exemplary shave,
how you can afford to be bold about the jugular
to whiffle thy razor shell scalpel keen.
Let us back to Wittenberg on any deadline's eve
alarm clocks blunt on the hide of our dreams
a bromance in the bibliotheque
to rip off the cacography left by yesteryear's geeks
towards a second-class with honours
and a job no-one kills for.

FOR STREET FIGHTERS

Sometimes I have at them with Ryu, the wanderer,
the gentleman, ideal for beginners,
barefoot and brutal in defence
Sometimes with Ken, pretty much the same
but easier on the eyes and with a cooler colour scheme.
I bet an opposable thumb your man is Sagat
that you spam his (↓↘→ + P) Tiger Shot
for fear I get within touching distance.
But no AI worth its pyjamas repeatedly falls for that,
I absorb your projectiles with projectiles of my own.
When I'm Akuma, I (→↓↘ + PPP) teleport to close the gap
cross you up and administer (LP LP ← LK HP) a 27 hit combo
where it goes dark and lo, lights out behind your eye patch.
Perchance you've the gumption to jump
Perchance I rock your scissors with a (→↓↘ + P) Dragon Punch,
EX Focus Cancel, a double tap ←←   to dash from your reach
follow it up with a (↓↙← + K) Hurricane Kick
and if my Revenge Gauge is lit, the (↓↘→↓↘→ + PPP) Metsu Shoryuken
to kill you dead with my atomic fist, the spectacle of a flashy background finish

Poem beginning with a line by Jacques Rivière

            —It is not being romantic
to say that pure thought has no issue other than death.
    Now swap death for wonder.
Suppose we boil it all down to this,
the world a gift horse we kiss on the mouth
    Condemn the banal to a burn barrel
I'd slough off my birthmark and colorectal polyps
but commuters would notice the burning and wonder
    Tonight let us start a tailback,
the M62 illuminations are free
the Yorkshire Rose suite yours to feng shui
    It's wonderful to séance with you in the bath
to adorn your fingers with Haribo rings
Imperial Leather, the ceramic surround
wonderful for sowing a five o'clock shadow in,
for Schwarzkopfing you Nordic blonde
    Come the morning buckle up for the news;
a gunshot in Haiti and nobody flinched
    Wonderful the horror that is to be missing
to be killed by someone who doesn't speak English,
the playgrounds euphoric with bratatat valour
wonderful their comic book onomatopoeia;
Sha!ting is a pot-shot-ricochet-off-kettle-hat
Spang! is a bullet caught in the teeth
but with Kevlar there's a thump
and silence for the bruise,
an ellipsis where wonderment goes
                Wonderful the stories
                that come with a cassette
                that beeps when it's time
                for turning the page.

                 n
                Me
                nn
               ha
            dp   a
            ed
               d 3 ye
            me
            pest
                the ab
        C a es   R n
        w o died   o
                d 54   ear
                also   of
                    n   isher
        wife   f Geo ge Fisher
                surgeon
        nd second daughter of
            RLES   AMSDEN
                died   oct 1915
            aged 65   ears

CHATTERBOX (TORN PAGE)

Johnny had got accustomed to the dim
ight now. One of the torches, flung to
he floor, was still glowing. By its light
e saw that the face he was about to
unch didn't need punching, for the mix-
o with the insides of the Cyclone had
one all the necessary damage. The
llow's face was a mass of blood, and
's hands fled to his eyes, which were half-
inded by oil off the engine.

    Johnny pushed him out of the way,
en turned to deal with the second man.
  ust in time, too! For that man was
ming around the Cyclone's bonnet at
ohnny. He had a spanner raised to
ash down on the lad's head.

  "No you don't!" the youngster gritted
and doubling like a hairpin, he dived
r his attacker's ankles. He took these
a lovely rugby tackle which bowled
s attacker over like a blitzed skittle.
xt moment Johnny was on top of him
mmering him for all he was worth.

    Vreck his Dad's car, would they?

cranial tissues!'
'It's a bump to me,' Bill told
'Call it what you like, it means the
thing. A hefty whack with a spanne
'Did they damage the Cylco
Johnny asked, sitting up.
'Not so you'd notice, thanks to
Bill grinned. 'You arrived just in
They took me unawares, and I had
chance. They had me tied up and ga
before I could say 'Sparking B
I'd a heck of a job to get loose after th
gone.'
'Did they beat it after knockin
out?' Johnny asked.
'Like scared rabbits!' They se
to think you were an army!'
'I was mad enough for anyth
Johnny agreed. 'What now?'
'You get off to sleep,' Bill
'I'll stay awake, although I don't
they'll come back after th
about you gave 'em!'
Truth to tell,

ELSEWORLDS #1

Summer of '47. Roswell, New Mexico,
a ranch hand gawps at some kinda crash site.
It breaks his heart, what them Reds could intern
and shoot into space, squeezing his thumb
with a scaffolder's grip,
tantrum of a colossus
in the astral crib.

Flashforward to '62,
Kennedy to mobilise the blue boy scout
full-throttle cobalt at a million dots per inch
emblem embroidered in Pepsi-Cola script,
a fatherly noogie and the good to go.
He can keep the brinkmanship up all night.

Charlie's gonna burn, faster than a paper tiger.
In the morning, the smell of heat vision
like no victory of this earth.

From a prospective Russian bride

Ave, my gentleman,
life is what we make of it.
It is never too late to fall in love
to socialise as it helps me understand life,
to travel as it broadens me out.
I love animals, different types
of music, sport,
driving cars, hot countries,
expensive fragrances.
As a sweetheart I am still
waiting for a man who has quiet power,
the type of man who would become bedfellows with
the only surviving son of the late lieutenant colonel J Garang Hinga.
As a sweetheart I am still
waiting for the man who will take me to an arcade
and teach me to shoot inside the screen.

A Guide for Aspiring Blade Runners

1

She need not be pretty per se, so long as her eyes can smile
and she blinks from time to time

a hand always ready for the fall of an apple
and all the things of yours that could be broken

She will take the glasses off your face
fold and place them on the bedside table

to begin a tiny decoupage
kiss by kiss wherever they count

her saliva in your mouth a hardcore vinaigrette
your tongues like an exorcism of flukes

zero possibility of miniature hands
their shadows an owl on the walls of her womb.

2

He doesn't watch through the eyes of whoever got the drop on him
but respawns in time to catch his old body and lay it to rest

a regime of entertainment that requires him to kill
to scalp something less yielding than a head of steamed milk

and regard his own head as long since struck off
pride of place upon a battlement in heaven

so it has no part in whatever his body is ordered to perpetrate
feng shui of such excessive misalignment

a mission to unhorse the villain of the day; Vladimir Putin,
Richard the Third, the net effect of their time on earth

horror that makes the heart reach up
to the throat for some air time.

3

Raoul Moat, ripped and heavy-jowled
raises his voice to scream

his scream a javelin
impales the crust of local bucolic

Cue the manhunt, owing to austerity
in pitch-black where possible

by day, the same stretch of England
on loop in each shot

rain in the direction of an enraged forward slash
as police convene to sweep away

a banquet only such weather would peck
the prospect of a six-pack and chicken with Gazza.

SHE WAITS IN GOOGLE

she waits
she waits **for me**
she waits **to text me back**
she waits by **the window**
she waits by **the sliprails**
she waits by **the well**
she waits by **the door**
she waits by **the wall**
      by the **bridge**
      by the **rivers**
      by the **way**
      by the **by**
      by the **pricking of thumbs**
      by the **rivers of Babylon**
      by the **beach**
      by the **horn**

she waits for you **to go to sleep**
she waits for you **at the top of the tower**
she waits for you
always she waits for you
浜田省吾 she waits for you
      for you **a thousand times over**
      for you **alone lyrics**
      for you **alone chords**
      for you **and your denial**
      for you **are in elysium**
      for you are in **elysium and already dead**
      for you she **was a chapter**
            she was a **phantom of delight**
            she was a **girl from birmingham**
            she was a **skater girl**
            she was a **spinning glass heart**
            she was a **hurricane**

she waits for me
she waits for me **after class**
she waits for me **in hell**
she waits for me **ever so patiently**
she waits for me **outside a hole in the ground**
she waits for me **to call**
she waits for me **to text her**
        to text **or not to text her**
                what to text her **after a date**
                what to text her **when she doesn't reply**
                what to text her **the next day**
                what to text her **to make her laugh**
                what to text her **to get her back**

and now she**'s gone**
and now she**'s two years older**
and now she**'s far far away**
and now she**'s dancing with another man**
and now she **was colder by the hour**
and now she **back from outer space**
and now she**'s back in the atmosphere**
and now she**'s calling a cab**
and now **a word from our sponsor**
and now **the end is near lyrics**
and now **his watch is ended**
and now **the screaming starts**

she waits in **the restless horizon**
she waits in **November**
she waits in **and out of Texas**
        in a waiting **room**
        in a waiting **line**
        in a **boxcar** waiting
        in a **world like this**
        in a**pp purchase**
        in a**rrears**
        in a **new york minute**
        in a **nutshell**
        in a **broken dream**

She waits in IMDb.com

A lone woman stands on the side of a desolate road. She appears to be concerned, confused and lost. / She waits half the day for help, but when the massive truck pulls in behind her, she begins to feel something is very wrong. / In a waiting room of an airport, a young lady is eating crackers while she's waiting for her flight. / While she's waiting to leave, she acts as our guide as we travel into the lives of her flatmates, her boyfriend's band, her family and few complete strangers who have nothing to do with anything (probably). / A young girl who has lost her love to the sea (in more ways than one) can't seem to get her life off hold as she waits for him to return. / She spends her days lulling a doll in her arms as she waits for her love to rise from the depths. / As she waits for her husband to return, she occasionally spends time with her friend Bernadette, whose presence makes the long winter bearable. / She spends six years raising her daughter alone while she waits for her husband to return from overseas. / She waits tables. / She waits for the end of the world. / She waits in front of the door. / While she waits with dinner ready, imagine several scenarios to enjoy together. / She's waiting for a special prince to sweep her away. / She is waiting for Jóska at the train station of a small Ukrainian town. / She is waiting with a meal. / She is waiting at the train station with coffee and serious doubts. /

She is waiting for the train to arrive when a mysterious and soaked man shows up. / Chained up in Hell, she is waiting for her boyfriend to rescue her. / She waits for him in the confines of the cult's lascivious leader / holding onto the promises that he made and the belief that he would never abandon her. / She is waiting on a train, he is waiting for answers. / As she waits for her train, the stranger lurks nearby on the platform, so that he can make sure to sit in the same carriage as her. / With every struggle to catch her breath, we feel more deeply her pain and helplessness as she waits for the miracle that destiny may never deliver. / While she waits for her train, the young woman finds herself slowly captivated by the alluring text messages of a secret admirer. / After her pals can't dissuade her, they insist on going with her to the trendy bar where she waits to get picked up. / Gleefully hooked on her dangerous new plaything, she waits for her little game to end. / She gives him an ultimatum that if he leaves she will not be waiting for him when he returns. / She is waiting for surgery that can restore her eyesight. / She waits till Tim (as he said in the letter) would come later in the evening. But he does not come. / When she tells him that she is pregnant and that she will wait for him, he has no other choice but surrender. / They plan to leave the country together, but at the airport she waits for him in vain. / Locked in her self-imposed exile, she waits for the right moment to step back into the world and claim what is hers and hers alone.

HAPPY THE CHILD WITH DISPERSED WHITE LIGHT

Happy the child with dispersed white light,
on whose authority I have it that there's only one horizon,
that it's not like hurdles you can jump over, silly
and it will remain pig-headed
in its refusal to meet us halfway.
It takes a real jerk to deny a child paper
but her mum and I, we need to tighten our belts,
so for what remains of the poem
she will have to be seen by the lights of her eyes
darting to and fro upon a plain black screen
with the occasional owl noise
to represent a toilet trip in the night,
overseeing a sloeblack Sylvania
where everyone says hello to everyone,
releases fairies with all legs accounted for
and describes the book I'm reading
as being too fat.

POETUI (FOR THE POET)

Henrikas Radauskas—a translation

Like a sun amidst the cosmos cinders
Cooling in the shade of neutron stars—
You'll find yourself, calm in solitude
Within your poems' degenerate matter.

The drone of planets before their demise
Like bluebottles trapped in a cobweb.
And you, who put no stock in eternity,
And your works, their breath no longer visible,
Slowly encased in a reliquary of ice.

WALT WHITMAN IN MY POCKET

When she took her hand from mine
to point at the sky and ask what it is

it is the poetry mum warned me about
a fresh of breath air, the sky

at its best is (without limitation)
a layered drink, a pousse café

octopus ink in a grey cornea
Bob Hoskins' face

at the end of *The Long Good Friday*
In other words, look how much goes on in there

TRIHAYWBFRFYH

after Connor Sherlock

The Rapture Is Here
And You Will Be Forcibly Removed From Your Home
And You Will Make A Beeline for Ramshackle Dwellings In Hope Of
       An Off Button
And You Will Lack The Hands With Which To Turn The Door Handles
       You Happen Across
And You Will Be Compelled To Run Until You Reach A Fence
And You Have To Walk Crestfallen All The Way Back Into The Shadow
       From Which You Were Running
And You Will Prefer To Spend Your Last Twenty Minutes Curled Up In
       A Ball,
Your Head In A Paper Bag That Smells Like Your Takeaway Of Preference
And You Will Wonder Why You Didn't Notice These Peculiar Objects
       When Last You Traversed This Blasted Heath
(Or Are There Mind Games Afoot In The Rapture?)
The Rapture Is Here
And You Will Have To Face Up To It;
Your Misbegotten Sense Of Gamer Entitlement
There Is Nothing In The Rapture You Can Left-Click To Death
And To Think You Tapped Your Phone For Entire Commutes
Just To Keep A Little Man Running
When There Is So Much Out There We Can Stroll Towards
In Our Own Time, At Our Own Pace
On a Day Like Today
But Without The Rapture

Gareth Durasow was born in Pontefract in 1984. He grew up in Castleford and studied in Leeds and Huddersfield, where he now lives. His friend and mentor, the artist David Prudhoe, once lent him a stack of poetry collections to keep him busy whilst in hospital. He has been busy ever since, with his own poetry appearing in publications throughout the UK, Europe and the US.

He teaches English, ESOL and Creative Writing for Wakefield Adult Education Service.

ND - #0523 - 270225 - C0 - 229/152/6 - PB - 9781907133909 - Matt Lamination